The Wanderers

Anna Ziegler

methuen | drama

LONDON • NEW YORK • OXFORD • NEW DELHI • SYDNEY

METHUEN DRAMA
Bloomsbury Publishing Plc
50 Bedford Square, London, WC1B 3DP, UK
1385 Broadway, New York, NY 10018, USA
29 Earlsfort Terrace, Dublin 2, Ireland

BLOOMSBURY, METHUEN DRAMA and the Methuen
Drama logo are trademarks of Bloomsbury Publishing Plc

First published in Great Britain 2023

Cover design by Rebecca Heselton

Brick texture © Unsplash; figures © Good Studio/robuart/shutterstock

A catalogue record for this book is available from the British Library.

A catalog record for this book is available from the Library of Congress.

ISBN: PB: 978-1-3503-9855-9
ePDF: 978-1-3503-9856-6
eBook: 978-1-3503-9857-3

Series: Modern Plays

Typeset by Mark Heslington Ltd, Scarborough, North Yorkshire

To find out more about our authors and books visit
www.bloomsbury.com and sign up for our newsletters.

The Wanderers was originally developed and produced by The Old Globe (Barry Edelstein, Artistic Director; Michael G. Murphy, Managing Director). It opened on April 13, 2018, at the Old Globe Theatre (San Diego) in the Sheryl and Harvey White Theatre with the following cast and creatives:

Esther	**Ali Rose Dachis**
Schmuli	**Dave Klasko**
Abe	**Daniel Eric Gold**
Sophie	**Michelle Beck**
Julia	**Janie Brookshire**
Director	Barry Edelstein
Stage Manager	Anjee Nero
Scenic	Marion Williams
Costume	David Israel Reynoso
Lighting	Amanda Zieve
Sound	Jane Shaw
Projections	Jeanette Oi-Suk Yew

The Wanderers had its New York premiere at the Laura Pels Theatre in the Harold and Miriam Steinberg Center for Theatre directed by Barry Edelstein on January 26, 2023, produced by Roundabout Theatre Company.

Thank You

Firstly to Danielle Mages Amato, without whose wisdom and encouragement during the development of this piece it would surely not exist.

To the Old Globe Theatre—Eric Keen-Louie, Justin Waldman, and of course Barry Edelstein, whose incisive and wholehearted vision for the play gave it first life and breath.

To Jill Rafson, Todd Haimes, and the Roundabout Theater for their belief in this piece and for sticking with it through years of pandemic-related delays.

To the brilliant Daniel Eric Gold, Michelle Beck, Ali Rose Dachis, Janie Brookshire, and Dave Klasko for making all of the discoveries bravely and beautifully in front of our first audiences.

To Amber McGinnis, Sarig Peker, Tyne Rafaeli, Stefan Kroner, and the Ernst Deutsch Theater Hamburg; Clare Drobot and City Theatre; Roy Chen, Amir Wolf, and the Gesher Theater; Adam Immerwahr and Theater J, and many many others for helping to shepherd this play into the world.

And to Will, Elliot, Nathaniel, Richard, and Carolyn for all the rest.

The Wanderers

For my parents and my children

L'chi Lach to a land that I will show you
Leich L'cha to a place you do not know
– Debbie Friedman

Tell me, what else should I have done?
Doesn't everything die at last, and too soon?
Tell me, what is it you plan to do with your
one wild and precious life?
– Mary Oliver

There is always a suspicion . . . that one is living a lie
or a mistake; that something crucially important has
been overlooked, missed, neglected, left untried and
unexplored; that a vital obligation to one's own authentic
self has not been met, or that some chances of unknown
happiness completely different from any happiness
experienced before have not been taken up in time
and are bound to be lost forever.
– Esther Perel

The poet appears to have found his subject—the labyrinth
of self-deceit into which we are led by, among other
things, language itself, by the difficult reformulation
of one's own story.
– Margalit Fox, "J.D. McClatchy, Poet of the Body, in Sickness
and Health, Dies at 72," *The New York Times*

Characters

Esther, *mid-twenties–early thirties; she feels young, impressionable, eager and yet no-nonsense too; she's Jewish (Hasidic).*

Schmuli, *thirties—formal, not totally comfortable in his skin, also Hasidic; should have the capacity for deep, surprising emotion; he is a profoundly gentle person.*

Abe, *mid-thirties–early forties—an intellectual who knows he's an intellectual, enjoys seducing with language, a bit pretentious but charming and not without humor and self-awareness/self-deprecation; he is Caucasian, Jewish.*

Sophie, *mid-thirties–early forties—Abe's wife, dry and intelligent and world-weary; she is biracial: Caucasian/Jewish and Black.*

Julia Cheever, *mid-thirties–early forties—a movie star with an abundance of outward charm and confidence and an easy laugh; she is poised and polished, but not without vulnerability.*

Time: 1973–1982 and 2015–2017.

Place: Williamsburg, Brooklyn and Albany, New York.

Sophie *stands in a spotlight. Perhaps behind a lectern, at a reading.*

Sophie   I was seventeen when I realized I was going to marry Abe. We were driving home from school. I was driving because Abe, even then, was too neurotic. What if he crashed the car and was responsible for something terrible? So I drove. And on this particular day he was reading aloud. This wasn't unusual. Abe loved to read to me. Mostly his own writing, but also passages from his favorite novels; once, at a Foot Locker, he recited the last lines of Philip Roth's *Sabbath's Theater* over and over again, laughing and then . . . crying. "And he couldn't do it. He could not fucking die. How could he leave? Everything he hated was here." And the guy who worked there was looking at me, like "Are you sure you're okay?" But I was. And I bought these bright pink high-tops to make my mother worry she would never really know me and to make Abe think I was bold. The day I realized I was going to marry him, we were in the car and he was reading a poem of mine aloud. A poem he'd grabbed out of my backpack, against my will. But the way he read it, with so much reverence for each word, made it sound . . . beautiful. And important. And I felt completely . . . seen.

Beat.

I was almost forty when I realized I would leave him.

Chapter One (or, Marriage)

Enter **Esther** *and* **Schmuli**, *dancing, but not together; they stay separate from each other. We are at their wedding. There is something frantic and beautiful about the dance.*

Then it is just after the wedding. Late at night. **Esther** *and* **Schmuli** *are alone together for the very first time.*

Esther   So how did you enjoy our wedding?

Schmuli (*not sure how to answer*)   I thought it was very . . . pleasant.

Esther   Yes. It was.

Schmuli   Did you enjoy the dancing, I wonder?

Esther   I wish! All I could think about was keeping this sheitel on; I was praying so hard that it wouldn't fall off.

Schmuli   But it didn't?

Esther (*wryly, with a smile*)   What a merciful God we have, right?

Beat. They both look at the ground.

Esther   I'm sorry. Usually I have a lot to say. Usually people tell me, "Enough already, Esther."

Schmuli   You did talk a lot. At our meeting.

Esther   I was so nervous! My Tante Golde said, "You're twenty-three, practically dead. If this one isn't a match, you're done for." (*Smiling.*) I guess I can tell you that, now that you're stuck with me.

Schmuli   I'm very pleased to be stuck with you.

Esther   You're sweet. I could tell you were sweet. What could you tell about me?

He doesn't say anything, looks down.

Esther   You must've thought *something*.

Schmuli   I thought you had very nice shoes.

Esther   Nice shoes.

Schmuli   Yes.

Esther (*a genuine question, gentle*)   What, did you never look at me?

Schmuli (*reassuring, kind*)   And yet I saw enough.

Esther   You might be crazy, Schmuli Simcha. To marry without even looking.

Schmuli Not crazy. Only shy.

Esther And what happens now.

Schmuli Oh, I um . . . I mean, we don't have to, um.

Esther No—I didn't mean *now* now. I know what happens *now* now.

Schmuli You do?

Esther I meant in life. Like is this moment the beginning of the rest of our lives?

Schmuli Isn't that true, every day?

Esther (*hopeful*) Does it feel that way to you?

Schmuli Maybe we should just focus on what happens now. One never really knows what anything means. At least not till so much later.

Esther I see.

Schmuli It's not just that I only want to . . . um.

Esther Have you ever done it before?

Schmuli (*shocked at the question*) Of course I have not done it; what kind of a question is this?

Esther I have read books about it. I've read books I probably shouldn't have read.

Schmuli I have a feeling it's different in life than in books.

Esther How so?

Schmuli I don't know. When I listen to music I don't have the experience of listening to music that I've read about. And . . . I've listened to music I probably shouldn't have listened to.

Esther (*excited that they are both rebellious*) How do you experience listening to music?

Schmuli It depends on the music, of course, but.

Esther   But?

Schmuli   It's the closest I've ever come to God.

Esther   Closer than during Neilah, when the gates are closing?

Schmuli   Yes.

Esther   Well, they say . . . relations between a man and a woman are also supposed to bring one closer to God.

Schmuli   They do say that.

Esther   I'm not eighteen years old, you know. I'm not scared.

Schmuli (*even more terrified*)   So you would like to simply . . . commence, then?

Esther (*not rude but surprised*)   Is that how you're going to ask me?

Schmuli   I don't know . . . How *should* I ask you?

Esther   . . . Why don't you say my name.

Schmuli   Esther.

Esther   Yes . . . Say my name and then say . . . (*She thinks.*) Say: "come to me."

Schmuli (*awkward*)   Esther. Come to me.

Esther   No, it doesn't sound right. Can you think of anything?

Schmuli   How about "are you ready to commence?"

Esther   You did that one already.

Schmuli   Did I?

Esther   Yes.

Now we meet **Abe**, *who's on a total high. He and* **Sophie** *are at home, in Brooklyn.*

Sophie   She didn't really write to you.

Abe   Look: yes-its-me-the-real-julia-cheever at gmail.com.

Sophie   That isn't really her. That can't be her actual email address.

Abe   Sure it is. She's being ironic. And I know you'll laugh at me, but I'm not entirely surprised that she wrote. I mean, she sat right up front at the reading. She wanted me to see her. She was engaging me, somehow.

Sophie   Yes I will laugh at you.

Abe   Well, if you didn't laugh mercilessly at me everyday I'd think something was terribly wrong.

Sophie   Let me see the email.

Abe   It's private.

She shoots him a look—she's not messing around. He hands **Sophie** *his laptop.*

Then: **Julia Cheever** *in spotlight.*

Julia   Dear Abe—can I call you Abe? I hope it's not wrong of me to write. Or presumptuous.

But I heard you read last week and I haven't been able to stop thinking about it. James, my husband, is one of your biggest fans, and I admit—he dragged me along with him. I don't usually go to book readings. As you can imagine I can't go anywhere in public without a hassle—

Sophie   Seriously? She can't go anywhere "without a hassle"? Come on.

Abe   Well, it's probably true.

Sophie   Also it *is* kind of presumptuous, don't you think? Just to write you, out of the blue.

Abe   Except she's not wrong. I was thrilled to hear from her.

Sophie   You really think she's that pretty?

Abe (*matter-of-fact*)   Luminous.

Sophie   Please don't hold back on my account.

Julia   And also, and really more to the point, aren't most book readings mind-numbingly boring? But not yours. And I would say I loved what you read—which I did—but even more I loved what you *said*. About the never-ending conflict between the head and the heart, between the private and the public self, between what we think we want and what we actually have. I found you very . . . appealing. Is that wrong of me to express? Well, screw it—that's how I felt. And I know you've been accused of writing unlikeable characters but I'll say this—if your characters are anything like you, then I think your critics are wrong.

Then a change in tone—lighter.

Anyway, I guess I'll read your books now. Or at least add one to the stack on my bedside table, so I'll always be *about* to begin. Ha ha. Yours sincerely, Julia

Sophie   And you really think that's her.

Abe   You don't?

Beat.

Or you just don't believe Julia Cheever could find me appealing?

Sophie   Yeah, both. I don't think it's her and I don't think she would find you appealing.

Abe   Really, the danger now, for you, is that someone on the list is actually within reach.

Sophie   I'll remember to be worried, thank you.

Abe (*joking*)   You know what? I'm feeling generous. I think I'll let you have Dan Rather. He took such a shine to you at that NEA luncheon.

Sophie   Oh, I'd take Brokaw over Rather.

Abe   Sure, that gravelly voice, that wholesome Midwestern trustworthiness. Like so many men of a certain era. Whereas Julia Cheever could only be Julia Cheever. She doesn't seem like anyone else.

Sophie   You don't know her. You know that, right?

Abe   Let's go dancing.

Sophie   We don't go dancing. That is not something that we do.

Abe   But we could. Wouldn't it be nice to do something novel? Maybe we could even drink and do drugs.

Sophie (*scoffing*)   "Do drugs."

(*Then, interested.*) Which drugs?

Abe   I don't know. Nicotine. What do you say?

Sophie (*snapping her fingers*)   Oh, shoot. I just remembered those small children sleeping in the other room. We can't leave them in the house alone. It's frowned upon by the law and also they might kill each other.

Abe   Right. Fine. Then do you want to have sex?

Sophie (*without missing a beat*)   No.

Abe (*also without missing a beat*)   Okay.

Sophie   I'm gonna go to bed.

Abe   Already?

Sophie   . . . I have kind of a big day tomorrow.

She stares at him, pointedly.

You have no clue what I'm talking about.

Abe   No. I do.

Sophie   Then what. What am I doing tomorrow?

He kisses her tenderly on the cheek.

Abe   Have I told you how much I love you? That I couldn't survive without you?

Sophie   I have a meeting with that editor.

Abe   Yes! Of course. The meeting with the editor. The young one, right?

Sophie   Well, it's a new imprint.

Abe   . . . So you're going to write another book. That's the plan?

Beat.

Sophie (*touchy*)   I don't know, Abe. I don't know if I'll write another book. It's just a meeting.

Abe   Well, you don't have to. If you don't want to.

Sophie   Thanks for that.

She turns to go.

Abe   No, don't go.

Sophie (*suddenly cutting*)   Are *you* gonna write another book?

Beat.

Abe   Why wouldn't I?

Sophie   Exactly.

She exits; **Abe** *immediately writes back.*

Abe   Julia Cheever. I didn't really believe it when I saw your name in my inbox, like an answered prayer. My wife assumed it was a hoax. But who would know that I've admired you so all these years? So I won't over-think things, as is my wont. Also, for the record, it's *women* I'm accused of making unlikeable. Apparently I couldn't recognize a real woman if she was staring me in the face.

Chapter Two (or, Children)

Schmuli *and* **Esther** *are in her hospital room. She's recently given birth to their first child, who is in a bassinet next to her bed.*

Schmuli   I am just . . . amazed really. *Hodu L'Hashem Kitov Ki Leolam Chasdo.*

Esther (*looking down at the baby, overwhelmed/humbled*)   I know . . . It's incredible.

Schmuli   And you . . . I mean, you were so . . . I was so impressed.

Esther   You weren't even in the room!

Schmuli   One moment you were shrieking so loud I thought my eardrums would burst—

Esther   Okay, I'm not so sure I need to relive all that—

Schmuli   And I was reciting the Psalms over and over again—

Esther   You did say those Psalms an awful lot. I could hear you.

Schmuli   Psalm 20 is thought to be particularly good for easing the pangs of labor. Nine verses for nine months of being with child. Seventy words for the seventy pains of labor.

Esther   Were there only seventy?

Schmuli   I must've recited them fifteen times.

Esther   You must have.

Schmuli   My mouth got tired. My tongue was very dry.

Esther   I'm sorry your mouth got tired and your tongue was dry.

Schmuli   I didn't want to take any of your ice chips; you seemed in desperate need of them.

Esther   Do you want to hold her?

He keeps a certain distance away.

Come on; she won't bite. No teeth.

Schmuli   But is it permitted?

Esther   She's your daughter, Schmuli. Who cares if it's permitted?

Schmuli   . . . No, she's sleeping. I won't disturb her. God willing there will be much time for me to hold her. Our little little. Our *n'shomela*.

Esther   *Ein ba'al ha-nes makir b'niso.*

Schmuli   It's true. We are very blessed.

Esther   Should you go daven? It's late.

Schmuli   Yes.

But he doesn't move.

Esther   What is it, Schmuli. *Nu?*

Schmuli   I wonder if you feel the same as you did before. Or if God has moved through you so that now you are filled with his light.

Esther (*laughing a little*)   "Filled with light?" No, I feel tired! That's what I feel.

Schmuli (*chastened*)   Okay.

Esther (*then, gentler*)   No. I mean, of course it is a miracle. Here is this baby, and I don't know where she came from. But also, at the same time, the pain, and I'm sorry, but the blood, and I threw up on the doctor's shoes, and there were so many instruments inside me I was like an orchestra. So, no . . . it wasn't just light and holiness, Schmuli. I'm sorry.

Schmuli   No, *I'm* sorry. I know I never say the right things.

Esther (*gently*)   Just go daven. Tell the family and receive their blessings.

Schmuli   Okay, I will. But Esther.

Esther   What?

Schmuli   Can I just say . . . The thing I was going to say . . . the thing I wanted to say . . .

Esther   Go on.

Schmuli   One moment you were shrieking and the next moment . . . there she was, and the way she cried out was like a song, like a question, and the answer was: yes, I will care for you the rest of my life.

The lights shift. **Julia** *and* **Abe** *are emailing.*

Julia   Holy shit, Abe, you wrote back! It made my day. I'm sitting in my trailer, on the set of *Everyman*—the new Philip Roth adaptation—just glowing. Certainly not because of the content of the movie, which is as bleak as you would expect, but because there was some part of me that presumed you wouldn't have any interest in me. I don't have your way with words, after all.

Abe   Come on. You have all the *other* things. All I've got are words. And even those fail me much of the time. A relevant example: in the hours since receiving your email I've composed fourteen different responses. Any that tried to play it cool failed miserably. I can't pretend I'm not fascinated by everything about you. And I don't mean the being famous part, though of course I'm interested in that too, but mostly it's the daily stuff. How a presumably regular person lives this irregular life. How you have a marriage and two children—and please forgive me for knowing more about you than I should but I think it would be an insult to feign ignorance when all any of us should be doing with our time is following your every move. I am kidding, of course. Mostly. Though not about wanting to know who you are. I suppose the question is: how do you get through the day, Julia Cheever?

Sophie   Hey, so.

Abe *looks up, shifts his focus. There's* **Sophie**.

Abe   Oh, I didn't see you there. Did you put the kids to bed?

Sophie   Who else would have?

Abe   Is that like a dig?

Sophie   So I need to work tomorrow.

Abe   Okay.

Sophie   No, I mean, you'll need to wake up with the kids, make breakfast, take them to school, pick them up.

Abe (*matter-of-fact*)   You need to work all day?

Sophie   That's right. All day.

Abe   Let's just get a sitter then.

Sophie   I don't want to spend the next three hours trying to find a sitter. You can, if you want to. *Or* you can just not do your work for a bit tomorrow, and let me do mine.

Abe   What's going on, Sophie?

Beat.

Sophie (*embarrassed to bring this up*)   I'm not sure if . . . I mean, can I even call myself a writer anymore?

Abe   Of course you can.

Sophie   Even if I *never* do it? I don't know. Everything is just so simple for you—

Abe   Nothing is simple for me.

Sophie   You're right, getting a Pulitzer and two National Book Awards before turning thirty is pretty rough.

Abe   I can't re-read *A Theory of Milk* without wanting to kill myself. Its pretentiousness is staggering. And *Orphan of Vilnius* is a work of sheer genius (*he smiles*) but I'm still gonna die one day.

Sophie   Abe.

Abe   And before that be subjected to routine colonoscopies.

Sophie   I'm grinding my teeth again. This morning I woke up and it felt like there'd been a war in my mouth.

Abe   Like when Robby was born.

Sophie   And when my book came out . . . I mean, I worked so hard on it and for what?

Abe   It's an objectively beautiful book.

Sophie   It is. That's the tragedy of it all.

Abe   You did for Vietnamese villagers what Faulkner did for the American South.

Sophie   I researched the shit out of that novel.

Abe   It showed.

Sophie   What does that mean?

Abe (*not letting her goad him into a fight*)   Can I say something and not have you bite my head off? Something you already know.

Sophie   What.

Abe   It won't make you happy. The writing. Not ever.

Sophie   No, that's you, honey.

Abe   You will feel like someone else's book is better. You will feel misunderstood and underappreciated. You will feel certain your best work is behind you but even that wasn't good enough. You will feel like a failure no matter what so don't try to write what you think they want to read. You, Sophie, are so interesting. I mean—all the *inherited trauma*; how many people can claim a legacy of the Holocaust *and* slavery.

Sophie   But I don't want to write about myself. I write to get away from myself. Also, slavery and the Holocaust don't define me. I grew up in Albany. The only place I ever wanted to escape was that weird music camp my mom made me go to.

Abe   Well, you don't have to write about any of it explicitly.

Sophie   But I'm not even sure I wanna write! That's what I'm trying to say. I don't know what I want. Sometimes I even wonder if I might want another baby—

Abe (*not unkindly*)   I thought we'd settled this.

Sophie   I don't wanna *not* do something and then regret it later on.

Abe   You really wanna put ourselves through all of that again just because it might be theoretically nice to have more children around some abstract, future Thanksgiving Day table?

Sophie   But maybe it *would* be nice.

Abe   Come on, Soph. You think anyone with more than two kids is certifiable.

Sophie   I do. I really do . . . I'm just looking for something, I think.

Abe   I know. We all are.

Sophie   My mother says I enable you. That I'm scared to do my own work so I tell myself yours is more important. And she's right. So why do you let me do it? Because you're protecting me from getting hurt again or because it makes your life so easy?

Breath.

Abe   Both, probably. If I'm honest, probably both.

Back to emailing; days later.

Julia   How do I get through the day? Gosh, Abe, I don't know. Same as you I'd imagine. There's a little added glamor, which gets old quickly, and many additional difficulties that never do, but mostly it's the mundane stuff. My son Bishop is almost three; the baby, Essex, is six months old, and I feel very lucky to be their mom. I know that's cheesy as hell. But it's true. And James and I have been married ten years now. So a lot of that is about finding ways to re-see each other, if that makes sense.

Abe   Wow. I wish Sophie and I could "re-see" each other. Mostly our relationship is fueled by an unspoken competition around who reads the most features in the *New Yorker* in a given week and who the kids love more. Right now it's me, and she hates it. But it's easier to be a father. Mothers are supposed to be everything to everyone. I get points if I just, like, show up to dinner.

Julia   You're right—it is harder to be a mother. Cut your wife some slack. Tell your children to be nicer to her. Every time Bishop sees a suitcase he sobs. He doesn't make it easy for me to go away. Not that it should be easy to leave him.

Abe   Sure, the guilt is terrible. I feel guilty when I'm in the bathroom too long, let alone on a book tour. I can't even get myself on a plane, not since the kids were born. All I can think of is that second when you realize the thing is going down and you'll never see them again. That your final moments would just be full of this terrible self-recrimination about leaving them without a father.

Julia   But flying is safer than driving. Everyone knows that.

Abe   Oh, logic has absolutely nothing to do with the decisions I make. It drives my wife crazy.

Julia   Is she supportive? Of your writing?

Abe   Totally. And also not at all. It's tricky. She's a writer too; she published a novel a decade ago and it got dismal reviews and then disappeared, which was incredibly disheartening for her especially in light of my success . . . see, there is a small, or perhaps not so small, way in which my wife hates me, but also can't, and it tortures her.

Julia   Does she know we're writing to each other?

Abe   Oh.

Yes.

More or less.

Maybe not the *entire* extent of it.

But she teases me. She says I need this to stave off a mid-life crisis.

Julia   My husband thinks I'm trying to ingratiate myself to you so I can be in your next film adaptation.

Abe   Well, it's working.

Julia   Good.

Abe   You know . . . If a day passes and I haven't heard from you I get . . . jumpy. It's like I can't focus.

Beat.

Julia   Abe, I'm not sure what to . . .

Abe   No.

Ignore me.

I'm an idiot.

I'm just so enjoying becoming your friend.

I can't tell you what your movies have done for me.

All of them, but especially the ones when I was a teenager. Those were formative.

You were this girl my age who was so smart but also beautiful but also attainable.

You made things seem . . . possible. Even though my home life was so . . .

Julia   So . . . what?

Abe   Sophie would say a train wreck. I'd say it was complicated.

Julia   So you and Sophie knew each other when you were kids?

The lights shift. **Abe** *rehearses a speech.*

Abe (*to the audience*)   I don't think there was ever a time when I didn't know Sophie. We grew up together. Our *mothers* grew up together, Hasidic Jews in Williamsburg, Brooklyn. Mine escaped not long after she had me. Sophie's got out much earlier.

So Soph and I are the products of very particular women . . . Recklessly brave women.

After all, it's not easy to leave a sect like the Satmars. They'll cut you off; one by one they'll snip the delicate threads that constitute your identity. When I was a baby, my mother had nothing. So yeah, Soph and I met before memory. Before anything is recorded and turned into a story. We were best friends. We went to middle school prom together, where I tried the whole time to dance with Sarah Winters, a snub for which I have yet to be forgiven, and we'd have gone to senior prom too if Soph hadn't gotten Lyme Disease and been laid up for three weeks watching so much *90210* she cycled completely through loving Dylan and then Brandon and then back to Dylan again. I brought her chicken soup that was inedible because I made it myself. We got engaged on my twenty-seventh birthday.

Sophie (*entering*)   Huh.

Abe   What do you mean "huh"?

Sophie   For one thing—that was terrible, when I had Lyme disease. So don't glorify it.

Abe   Was I glorifying it?

Sophie   I don't know, Abe . . .

Abe That's never the start of something that ends well. It's never: "I don't know, Abe. I just think you're awesome."

Sophie It's always just . . . weird. To hear our story as this, like, sound bite. It feels fundamentally . . . dishonest.

Abe Because it is.

Sophie But like to casually mention our mothers in that way?

Abe These are patrons at the 92nd Street Y, not paid psychoanalysts.

Sophie I wish you *would* see a shrink. You know that.

Abe I already lead the most examined life of anyone I know. I don't think I could take much more.

Sophie All the dreams. And the fights you had with your mom. And the dreams about the fights you had with your mom. Religion was loaded for her so it's loaded for you. / I get it.

Abe (*that word is such an understatement*) Loaded?

Sophie But right now there's nothing actually holding you to it. So just believe or don't believe. It doesn't have to be such a big deal.

Abe Of course you think that. You're not Jewish.

Sophie (*they've had this discussion many times before*) I'm half Jewish, Abe.

Abe Okay but you don't think of yourself as Jewish. You weren't brought up that way.

Sophie Unitarian is kind of like Jewish.

Abe Our children wouldn't know from Jewish if it weren't for me.

Sophie I will never understand why you want to raise our kids in a religion you hate.

Abe Because that's what Jews do!

Sophie   I mean, do you really need a whole prepared answer about how we met?

Abe   Oh, they always ask how your life affects your art on these kinds of panels. And you, my *liebling*, are my whole life.

Sophie (*flirty*)   . . . Am I?

Abe   Can I tell you something?

Sophie   What.

Abe   I want us to re-see each other.

Sophie   Re-see each other.

Abe   I've been thinking about you.

Sophie   What kind of thinking?

Abe   Fantasizing.

Sophie   Abe.

Abe   No, I have been. I wanna . . . do things to you we've never done before.

Sophie   Like what?

Abe   Unspeakable things. Right now.

Sophie   Right now?

Abe   Yeah.

Chapter Three (or, Boredom)

Schmuli *enters, home from work.* **Esther** *is listening to the radio and shuts it off as soon as he enters, but not soon enough.*

Esther (*covering, a little eager*)   So the girls are asleep, finally. You should have heard Leah tonight—Why why why. Why do I have to go to bed. But *why* do I need sleep to grow big. Why do I need to grow at all, why can't I just stay a child? She's a little nudga with all her questions . . .

Schmuli (*toying with her*)   What were you listening to?

Esther   What?

Schmuli (*with affection*)   *Nu*, will you really deny it?

Esther   I wasn't listening to—

Schmuli (*interrupting*)   I hope it wasn't FM. FM is worse.

Esther (*smiling—she's caught him*)   How would *you* know that.

Schmuli   Do you listen to the radio often?

Esther   No . . .

(*Mischievously.*) Yes.

Schmuli   How often.

Esther   I get bored.

Schmuli   How often do you get bored?

Esther (*a new, fun idea*)   I'd like to get a computer.

Schmuli   What? What kind of *mishegoss* is this? No one we know has a computer.

Esther   Who says we can't be the first?

Schmuli   Also we can't afford a television.

Esther   How about I get a job and then we get a computer.

Schmuli   Okay you have gone off the deep end. *Gornisht helfn.*

Esther   Many women have jobs. Rachy Heschel works the reception desk at her husband's insurance agency.

Schmuli   It is run out of their tiny home. I think the desk might be the only place for her to sit all day.

Esther   I'm serious.

Schmuli   And will it end there, Esther?

Esther   What?

Schmuli   If you get a job. If we get a comupter, will it end there?

Esther   I don't know. I'm not a prophet. Also I don't *want* to know what life has in store. It's too boring that way. Also . . . I don't like listening to you chew your food, and at night your breathing keeps me awake. Sometimes I wish the breathing would just stop, which is not the same as wishing you dead, I swear. Also, how was your day? Has Rev Moshul's rash begun to fade? Did you get to have lunch outside in the park? I always think of you eating lunch in the park and I am sick with envy.

Schmuli   It is not so wonderful, eating in the park. The pigeons are aggressive and I *shvitz* like crazy.

Esther   You should get a lighter rekel.

Schmuli   Who can afford it?

Esther   With the money from my *job*, I will get it for you.

Schmuli   And who will take care of Leah and Miriam? No. Wait until our children are grown. Then maybe you get a job.

Esther   And spend the next fifteen years at the mercy of Faigy Gurkow who comes down every hour to ask if I smell gas? At which point we check her burners and as always they are off—no gas.

Schmuli   It will be as Ha-Shem wants it. This is how our parents, our grandparents, our great-grandparents all went.

Esther   Whose voice is coming out of your mouth? Yours? Or your father's? *Meyn schver*, who thinks my eyes should never meet his. Who told my *tateh* his contribution was not raised right—"contribution," Schmuli.

Schmuli   Well, *I* don't think of you that way.

Esther   You are under his thumb. You would never say a word against him.

Schmuli Why should I upset him?

Esther In the years when you were in Israel, after yeshiva, did you not see other ways of life?

He doesn't say anything.

You were sent there, were you not, because you were questioning things. So maybe our daughter takes after her father.

Schmuli Or her mother, more like.

One day, B'esras Ha-Shem, we will have a son and perhaps he will take after me.

The lights shift. **Abe** *and* **Julia** *are instant messaging.*

Julia Oh good, you're there.

I've been looking for you.

Abe Have you. Wow. How are you?

Julia The nanny is homesick and both kids are sick and I can't get cast by Terrence Malick to save my life and this morning I lost it at my assistant and she started to *cry*. So that's how I am.

Abe (*with total seriousness*) Holy shit you are, like, a terrible person.

Julia (*smiling*) Don't say that!

Abe No, I'm on your side. And you know what? I'll even take it upon myself to cheer you up. I am after all known for being very cheery.

Julia Are you?

Abe Not at all. But I like a challenge.

Julia Tell me something cheerful then.

Abe Okay . . . how about when something you assume will go terribly wrong is not a total unmitigated disaster. For me that would be . . . my books. Also my children. Also dental work.

Julia   Not bad.

Abe   A close second might be when a barber or Uber driver or dermatologist doesn't make me talk to them.

Julia (*with joking disbelief*)   Really? There are times when *you* don't wanna talk?

Abe   Oh my God, I never wanna talk. I can literally think of nothing better than seeing "can't make lunch today" pop up on your phone, which means you get to just stay home, and not talk.

Julia   But your children might be there and you might have to talk to them.

Abe   Robby I could do without—ha ha—but Esther is fun. She has ideas all of a sudden. She has a worldview. I don't know where it came from.

Julia   Esther's a pretty name.

Abe   Snow days! Those are cheery. I'm not sure I've ever been happier than those mornings in childhood when you'd wake up and suddenly have the whole day ahead of you . . .

Julia   Dark chocolate with sea salt. Margaritas with salt around the rim. Corn on the cob coated in salt. If you catch my theme . . .

Abe   Mozart's overture to *The Marriage of Figaro*. Anything by Art Garfunkel—I'm a total Garfunkel guy—or Jay-Z. I love Jay-Z.

Julia   How about when a Cate Blanchett movie bombs?

Abe   Has that ever happened?

Julia   But think of how it would feel if it did.

Abe   The last sentence of a book you love. Gossiping about a book you hate.

Julia   "The conductor raised his baton, and in that moment Isaac saw his own existence through new eyes, as though a tourist of the strange and beautiful topography that was his life. He would find some way to endure this happiness. The conductor lowered his baton . . . and Isaac played."

Abe   Oh my God.

Julia   I couldn't put it down.

Abe   I don't know what to, um . . . I'm overwhelmed.

Julia   I loved it. Every word. *I* was overwhelmed . . .

(*Really giving him this gift.*) I think you're a genius, Abe.

Abe   You. You are by far the cheeriest thing I can think of.

Beat.

Julia   What would your wife say if she knew you flirted with me so shamelessly.

Abe   That seems like a dangerous game to play. The what-would-my-wife-think-of-all-of-this game.

Julia   But you wanna play it.

Abe   Absolutely.

Julia   Well.

Abe   Of course I've given this some thought. And what I imagine she would think amounts to a kind of condescending pity that would extend into a grudging sort of acceptance or even permission. Like, if this is how Abe wants to get his jollies, he should just have at it.

Julia   She's a tough one, your wife.

Abe   That's putting it mildly.

Julia   She's very pretty, if that's not a weird thing to say.

Abe   I suppose it's only weird coming from one of the most beautiful women in the world, which is objectively true according to *People* magazine and every man I've ever met. I feel like I'm corresponding with Helen of Troy. "Why, what could she have done, being what she is? Was there another Troy for her to burn?"

Julia   What is that? The *Iliad*?

Abe   Yeats.

Julia   You're trying to impress me.

Abe   Of course. And would you believe me if I said it was the only poem I know? That I use it whenever I need to sound smart?

Julia   No.

Abe   You're right. I'm insufferable. I know lots of poems.

Julia   Show off.

Abe   Only when I feel out of my depth. I mean, I don't know why you're engaging in this . . . correspondence, or whatever we should call it. It's obvious why I am, even if it makes me into a bit of a cliché. But you. Talk about mixing with the hoi polloi. Every day I think: Is she done with me now?

Julia   . . . Not yet.

The lights shift.

Chapter Four (or, Rivka)

Esther *in a spotlight.*

Esther   My best friend Rivka was quiet and full of fantasies—just as I was. So many afternoons of our childhood turned into evening while we sat together and read. And yes, we got books from the library, even though it was forbidden. This is how I came to know Ramona Quimby and Winnie the Pooh, and later Josephine March, Elizabeth Bennet. Sometimes Rivka would sigh while reading and I'd say, "*nu*, what is it?" But one comes to see that it is very hard to explain a passage in a book that someone else has never read.

Rivka was so invisible in her home she could use it to her advantage; sometimes she would even go into Manhattan, to museums. And so it was that leaning over to tie her shoe in the Temple of Dendur, she met Harold. Harold was not Jewish. Harold was *African-American*. Harold taught environmental science at the University of Albany. Needless to say he did not fit in with the community. I heard the most shameful things said about it. Awful. So Rivka left. Off the *derech*. People said she'd lost it—*gornisht helfn*. But if Rivka and Harold don't have the most beautiful children in the world. And if Rivka is not one of the happiest women I know. I mean, if she's crazy, then sign me up for the asylum.

Once I persuaded Schmuli—never very difficult—to let me visit her. I was twenty-eight and pregnant with our third child. When I arrive, she won't let me help with anything, even though she has little Sophie, only one month in the world, and two older kids, who don't lift a finger. And one night, after the children are finally asleep, she pours herself a very full glass of wine and says she is no longer spiritual, but if she were she would create a blessing over *this*—and she takes a small circular case from a drawer. She says these are pills that stop the body from conceiving a child. I stare at them. She has had her last baby, she tells me, laughing. But I don't find it so funny. There will of course always be a last baby, but I'd prefer not to know that while I am nursing him, while I am holding him in my arms in the middle of the night. Rivka shrugs. "Willful ignorance. An abdication of your power. But suit yourself."

And one morning, while Harold cooks *bacon*, and the children read the newspaper—the children!—my friend asks me what I want. I say "No bacon for me, thank you" and she smiles—no, she meant in life. Out of life. Just then the baby kicks, and I know all of a sudden it is a boy, my first and only boy . . . my last child, and there he is, sitting at the table with me, an old man whom I will never know. He looks at me with sad eyes filled with all the things that happen after I am gone. He says to me: "*Mameh*, did you get the things you wanted?" I don't know how to respond. Who really understands whether or not they are happy?

The lights shift. **Julia** *and* **Abe** *are instant messaging.*

Julia   So I'm sure you know that *Everyman* just came out. And that it bombed. The press just *loathed* it. I always know how badly a movie has gone when I don't hear from anyone. But I thought at least I'd hear from you.

Abe   Okay. First of all, I don't read reviews.

Julia   Yes you do.

Abe   No, I don't. I couldn't care less about them. And for the record, I can't wait to see your movie. I mean, Julia Cheever and Philip Roth? I'm gonna watch it everyday. I'm gonna go to sleep to it and I'm gonna wake up to it. You *think* I'm kidding.

Julia   But, Abe, the movie really *is* bad—

Abe   No it's not. And also that's giving them way too much power.

Julia   Like you've ever been panned.

Abe   Julia, Google "Abe Hausman" and "overrated" and see what you find. People hate me. They hate every idea I've ever put into the world. Every word. They're offended by my very existence.

Julia   Right: Everyone's terrible. We all lose. This isn't helping.

Abe   I'm sorry.

Julia (*ignoring him*)   I mean, Roth adaptations are never any good. But I thought this one was reaching for something more interesting. How Everyman leaves wife after wife in search of . . . what? In the end he's just left with all this regret about spending his life on these failed families instead of pursuing his art. He decides, at a certain point, to paint a painting and it's the first time we see him *smile*. So doesn't that mean it's a valid choice, sometimes, to be selfish?

Abe   *Of course* you have to be selfish. I mean, truly, what is there in this world to have faith in *besides* the self? Certainly not humanity, which is filled with real cruelty and the performance of cruelty, and death. Certainly not God—how can anyone believe in him? The ultimate in unreliability—

Sophie (*from offstage, interrupting him*)   Abe? . . . Abe? Where are you?

Abe (*to* **Julia**)   I have to go, but please don't feel bad. It would kill me to think you're out there feeling bad. You're amazing; you're a force of nature; you bring grown men to their knees. You're not capable of making anything that sucks.

Sophie *enters.*

Sophie   . . . What're you doing?

Abe   Working.

Sophie   Yeah. Me too. Wanna take a break?

Abe   Not really.

Sophie   . . . You in a groove or something?

Abe   Or something.

He doesn't say anything.

Sophie   What, you want me to go?

He gives her a genuine kiss on the cheek, apologetic.

Abe   Maybe we'll take a break a bit later?

Sophie (*hurt, but trying not to show it*)   Oh. Okay.

She leaves, then turns back.

Hey, how's Julia Cheever?

Abe   She's sad her movie was a bust.

Sophie   Oh. Poor her.

Yeah. It sucks.

Abe   I bet.

Sophie *leaves.*

Abe   Are you there?

No one responds.

Julia? Did I lose you? Julia?

The lights shift. **Schmuli** *in spotlight.*

Schmuli   One night, after working late, I walked home
from the office in new snow. It covered everything and was
still pure, the way a night snow is before morning. There is
no other way to say it—our little corner of the city felt full of
magic, as though Ha-Shem had swept through and touched
every forehead. "All is calm all is bright" goes the song; (*with a
knowing smile*) yes, I know it, and it was that sort of night—
mid-December. I wanted to stand on my tiptoes and whisper
"*kadosh, kadosh, kadosh*" into the sky. But all of a sudden I was
crying. Why? Because I realized in that moment that I never
felt this way in shul. What did *I* find holy? My wife's back as
she stood over the pots on the stove, trying not to overcook
anything. *Music.* Especially, I admit, Brahms, Beethoven . . .
Mozart. The faces of my little daughters, the way, when they
slept, you could see all the afternoons of your life.

Sophie   Abe. Abe, wake up.

She is gently shaking him, trying to wake him.

Schmuli   And then the doors to the shul opened and
released the men from evening prayers, still aglow with the
last words of the Amidah. In their hats and tallesem, and lit
by the snow under their feet, these most pious of our men
were a sea of black and white, as though things could be that
simple. My father was among them.

Sophie   Abe. Wake up. Wake up, honey.

Schmuli   Sometimes, when I was in Israel, I pretended I was someone else. An army man standing guard in front of a bank, a restaurant, a checkpoint. I mean what a *thing*, to hold a gun. If I ever have a boy, I would like for him to be less . . . gentle than I am. I would wish for him that his wife respects him. I would like him to be armed with words.

Sophie   Abe.

Abe   What is it? What time is it? I fell asleep.

Sophie   It got late. It's nearly six o'clock.

Abe   I'm sorry . . . I'm sort of . . . in a daze. I think I was having the strangest dream.

Sophie   Abe, your father died.

Abe   What?

Sophie   I'm so sorry. Your father died.

She is crying now, a little.

Abe   I don't understand.

Sophie   Your aunt left a message. He was out walking, she said. In the snow. He slipped. Apparently he'd been staring at the sky.

Abe   That's not possible.

Sophie   I know, it's . . .

Abe   No.

Sophie   Abe.

Abe   I can't comprehend it.

Sophie   I don't think you have to comprehend it right away.

Abe   . . . Maybe I should be alone. Should I be alone?

Sophie   If you want to be?

Abe   I think I want to be.

Sophie   Sure, whatever you . . . I'm so sorry, Abe.

She exits. **Abe** *sits with his thoughts. Soon he begins to rock back and forth.*

Abe (*under his breath . . . he has trouble remembering the prayer*) *Yitgadal v'yitkadash sh'mei raba . . .*

(*Starting over.*) *Yitgadal v'yitkadash sh'mei raba . . . b'alma . . .*

He puts his head in his hands. After a few moments he opens his eyes.

(*With desperation.*) Are you there? Are you there, Julia? I need you. Julia.

At first nothing—but then she appears.

Julia   Hey there, you. What's up?

Abe *lets out one great heaving sob.*

Abe (*quietly, more to himself*)   Behind my eyes all I can see is a black coat on the white snow, like a shadow of a man.

Julia   What's happened, Abe?

Abe   And I didn't even know him. Not really.

Julia   Know who?

Abe   I don't have any parents, I . . . (*And then realizing it.*) Oh my God, I don't have any . . .

He crumples.

Julia   Abe, you have me. You have people. You're not alone. Whatever's happened . . .

Abe   It's horrible, Julia. Life is short, and full of illusion. There is no order to be made from madness. I haven't said it before but I'm saying it now . . . I want to see you.

Chapter Five (or, Fathers and Sons)

Esther *is lying in a hospital bed.*

Schmuli (*excited*)   There is just so much to do!

Esther   Too much to do.

Schmuli   Don't worry, *mommellah*. I'll work out the details.
First the shulem zucher –

Esther   Okay, that is just for you to drink too much and
gossip with the men.

Schmuli   And eat peanuts! Don't forget the peanuts.

Esther   How could I.

Schmuli   The vach nacht the following night. And then the
bris of course. Three days later the shlishi lemilah.

Esther   There was none of this for the girls.

Schmuli   Exactly! This is a true celebration! Oh, if you
could have seen my father's face when I told him.

Esther   Was he happier than when Leah and Miriam were
born?

Schmuli   So much happier.

Esther *smiles, thinly.*

Esther   I don't know. Maybe we don't do all of it. Maybe we
don't follow every single rule for every single celebration.

Schmuli   No, no, we will do *every single* celebration. This is
my son! And then the celebrations around his first day in
cheder, first haircut, first lesson in Torah. His bar mitzvah!
Oh what a day that will be. The celebrations, they will never
end!

Esther   . . . Well I suppose you should enjoy it while it lasts.

Schmuli   What does that mean?

Esther (*offhanded, trying to be casual*)   I don't know for
certain that we will have more children.

Schmuli   Of course we will. Why wouldn't we?

Esther   I just don't know, Schmuli. If I want to.

I might like to go to school to become a librarian. I think it would be nice to spend my day surrounded by books.

Schmuli   *Goyishe* books!

Esther   There are ways to avoid having children, you know.

Schmuli (*pleading with her*)   But it is God's will that we have as many children as we can.

Esther   And yet there's a pill. One wonders: could it exist if God hadn't created it, too?

Schmuli   . . . Where is this all . . . No, you're tired. I shouldn't have come to talk to you at this particular moment. It can wait.

Esther   It's just conversation, Schmuli.

Schmuli (*impulsively, out of nowhere*)   My mother says the women talk about you, you know.

Esther   Is that right?

Schmuli   Yes.

Esther   Well, they talk about everyone. That's all the women do is talk.

Schmuli   I'll let you rest now.

Esther   No—wait. I have a name for our son.

Schmuli   Well, but we must consult with the rebbe first.

Esther   But I know it! It was my grandfather's. He fled the pogroms when he was a boy and came to America alone, with nothing, and still he made a life.

Schmuli   Come now, let's not be hasty—it must be approved.

Esther *speaks to the baby.*

Esther (*to the baby*)   Hello, Abraham. I'm your mother.

Schmuli   Well, now you've said it.

Esther (*quietly*)   And God said to Abraham: "*L'ech l'cha*. Go for yourself from your land to a land that I will show you."

Schmuli   Let his name be for a blessing.

Esther (*to the baby*)   But God went only partway with Abraham. The rest of the way he had to find on his own.

Schmuli   Esther—

Esther   *L'dor vador*. From generation to generation we go.

The lights shift.

Abe (*unhinged/fevered*)   So there's a scene in *Anna Karenina* where Kitty, Levin's wife, is giving birth, and at some point during the hours of her agonizing labor he realizes that what he's feeling is not unlike what he felt at his brother's deathbed. That these two experiences constitute "the loopholes" of life, through which you can glimpse something higher, something real. And, Julia, it's true. I mean, the sight of my father's body was like having a debate with someone who makes a point that suddenly obliterates your entire thesis. I looked at that body and I thought—well, you can't argue with that. At the funeral I stuck out like a sore thumb. I was surrounded by relatives I'd never met, who stared at me shamelessly as though I was to blame, but for what? I didn't know my father! Everything he did confused me, or scared me! Everything he said, everything he wore. Once he even took me to Williamsburg. I was eleven. And it's not like my dad and I went places together, or saw each other more than a couple times a year. On the way there he played classical music and at the end of each seemingly interminable piece, he'd say:

Schmuli   Did you like that, son?

Abe   And I'd nod. In Brooklyn we stayed in the car . . . He pointed out buildings that meant *nothing* to me.

Schmuli   That's Nachman the butcher's shop. There's Yos Perlov's grocery.

Abe   What was he trying to show me? Did he know me? Did he know I'd be drawn back there, so close I can almost touch it, that sometimes I cross Heyward Street and just stare at the men behind the beards, searching for what—myself? I mean, what if I was actually *meant* to live that life? It's not like the freedoms of this one bring me so much pleasure. Did he know me? That kills me, Julia. Even the possibility. Not that it excuses my awkward fumble around wanting to see you. Of course I can't blame you for not writing back. Has it been two months? Three? It feels like years. But I swear I never meant to inflict any real damage. Just to generate the kinds of small excitements that break up routines and give a person something to look forward to. And I wasn't gonna write this but then I figured what's the harm. Maybe I'll just keep writing to you—years of one-sided correspondence. Isn't that really what being a novelist is, anyway?

Sophie   Can I come in?

Abe   I'm sorry. I know I said I'd be down . . . an hour ago.

Sophie   It's fine. Your dinner's in the fridge.

Abe   You know how people say *Orphan of Vilnius* is this masterful tale of the cost of remembering—an allegory about the way the Holocaust is just lodged in our brains.

Sophie   They have said that, yes.

Abe   So I realize that for me the book just tells this small story. About this classical violinist—

Sophie   Isaac. The violinist of Vilnius. Try saying that three times fast.

Abe   Come on, Sophie, I'm working through something . . .

Sophie   Sorry, go on.

Abe   So yeah, his whole family is murdered before his eyes and what does he do to stop it? Nothing.

Sophie (*really asking*)   What could he have done?

Abe   And after the war, all he wants is to play the violin and he's absurdly talented; they want him at Carnegie Hall, at the Musikverein in Vienna, in London at Royal Albert Hall; and so he wanders the world for years, but he can't find God in any of those great halls and he can't grow up; he can't be anyone in the absence of his parents. He has no one to play for.

Sophie   I know you don't think so, but you're gonna be okay. You really will, you . . .

Abe (*quietly*)   That's what they said after my mother died.

Sophie   And haven't you been. More or less.

Abe   No. Never. Never okay.

. . . I know that sounds . . . ungrateful. But you know what I mean. You know it's not about you, or the kids.

Sophie   I know that. And they know that . . . But they miss you . . . Robby keeps asking when you two are gonna finish *Winnie the Pooh*. He won't read it on his own. He's *waiting* for you . . .

Abe *looks down, ashamed. Beat.*

Sophie   You're not your father, Abe. You're here.

Abe   *Hineni*. Here I am.

A breath. And then we're interrupted by **Esther**'s *cries/screams.*

Chapter Six (or, Destruction)

Esther   Where are they?

Schmuli, where are they?

Schmuli   Esther, please calm down.

Esther   Where are my girls, Schmuli, you tell me this instant.

Schmuli   They're just fine. Don't worry.

Esther   Don't worry? Their closets are emptied. Their things are gone. Even their beds are stripped. So don't tell me they're okay; tell me where they are.

Schmuli   I can't do that.

Esther   Yes you can. And you will. Right now.

Nothing.

Right now!

Nothing.

Okay, I will beg you. Schmuli tell me, please please tell me.

She gets down on her knees.

Schmuli!

Schmuli   Esther just . . . Please.

Esther   Your father did this.

Schmuli   No.

Esther   Your father's men then. Enforcers. And this way he can stand off to the side, holier than thou.

Schmuli   It's not like that.

Esther   No? Then you tell me what it's like.

Beat.

Tell me, Schmuli, or I will go crazy. I will scream in the streets. I will be very immodest.

Schmuli   But don't you see that that is where this has come from?! That you have brought this on yourself.

Esther   What?

Schmuli   All the books. And the radio. And the going outside without your stockings.

Esther   That was one time! I was pregnant in August. It was too hot!

Schmuli   And this talk of a pill to stop having children.

Esther   That was a private conversation. That was between you and me. Did your father find out about that?

Schmuli   I was curious if he'd heard of such a thing.

Esther   . . . Oh, Schmuli. No.

Schmuli   He is the person in our community to whom one goes about such things.

Esther   You fool. You *dumbkopf*.

Schmuli   You can't speak that way to me, Esther! I am your husband!

Esther   Then get our girls back. Get them back. Right now.

Schmuli   It's not that simple.

Esther   Where are they? I'll go and get them. I'll strap Abraham to my chest and bang down the door.

Schmuli   You are not to see them.

Beat.

Esther   For how long?

Beat.

No. No no no no no.

My babies, Schmuli.

Schmuli   Esther.

Esther (*suddenly calm*)   You see, I do the physical therapies with Leah every night for her limp.

I prepare Miriam her own dinner because she cannot tolerate any salt.

I read them to sleep otherwise they are afraid the *goyim* will kidnap them when the light is out.

They need me. I am their mother.

Schmuli   You should not have said that to me, about not wanting more children.

Esther   You *khazer*, I didn't mean take away the children I already have!

Schmuli   Don't say things you can't take back.

Esther (*dryly*)   And Abraham? He is only still here because he was in the hospital with me, being born?

Schmuli   He will join his sisters, as I understand it.

Esther   No. We're leaving.

Schmuli   You can't leave.

Esther   I am. I am taking Abraham and you can't stop me.

Schmuli   Don't be impulsive. You leave and you can never return. You will bring even more shame on the family.

Esther   What choice have you left me? To stay here and try in vain to get a glimpse of my children as they are picked up from yeshiva? To continue to live in your house and submit to the "mitzvah" with the man who stole away the only joy in my life? I cannot do it. I will not. No . . . You have not seen me from the moment we met. Not even once. If you had, you would not have allowed this to happen. This . . . destruction.

Schmuli   There was no stopping it, Esther. Once it started.

Esther   That is what a *nebech* says to justify his actions. A weak, weak man.

Schmuli   I am not weak! I mean, isn't it possible that I might agree? That even I felt you were taking things too far?

Esther   No you're just scared. Admit it.

Schmuli   I am! I *am* scared. I have a wife bent on tearing down the very walls that are keeping us safe!

Esther   All an illusion. There are no walls.

Schmuli (*unbroken and emotional*)   There are. And they're *here*. Out there, you're vulnerable—to everything. And you'll become just like everyone else. Succumbing to the petty temptations that destroy men's souls.

Esther   . . . Oh, Schmuli. We are already just like everyone else. Can't you see that?

The lights shift.

Julia   I'm sorry, Abe. For the long silence. And that you've been . . . struggling. It's not an excuse but I was on location for three months in Australia. My family was with me, and even though he and I barely saw each other, when I'd get home from the set there James would be, waiting for me, a glass of wine at the ready, like this eager, patient puppy. I felt terrible about it. So I hope you understand why I couldn't write to you, even though I wanted to.

Abe   Julia, reading your email was like hearing my name called while walking down a street in a foreign country where I didn't think anyone knew me. Or to be more physiological about it, I got tingles. Goose bumps. Why? Because—miracle of miracles!—not only did you suddenly reappear, but what a gift to know that our correspondence makes you feel guilty. Because if it makes you feel guilty there is something illicit about it, and if there's something illicit about it . . . Well, you get the gist. Please forgive my rejoicing at the good working order of your conscience. Not that I think we have anything to be ashamed of. We're just two adults approaching middle age with access to Wi-Fi who derive some small satisfaction from seeing what words the other one has to say.

Also, I think you're beautiful—luminous, even. But that goes without saying. When it comes to you.

Julia   Don't you wish you had a not very good working knowledge of a foreign language? I think it would be something not to know exactly what you're saying, or what others are saying to you. Sometimes I think we understand too clearly, you know?

Abe   Okay . . . so you didn't respond to my manifesto in celebration of your guilt.

Julia   I will admit there is a certain rush that comes along with getting an intimate look into someone else's life that you really have no right to. I think that's the source of any guilt, if it existed. And maybe we can leave it at that?

Abe   Quite right. And very sensible. A look into someone's life. Yes. But not just anyone's—someone whose work could bring chills, and who seemed to be speaking directly to you from far away.

Yesterday I was reading the Class Notes section of my college's alumni magazine where the secretary of the oldest class made a plea to classmates now well into their nineties to write in with news. "So much is still left unsaid," he wrote— which struck me. After all those years what could still be unsaid, unspoken?

And I found myself writing an entry about my life now, full of things best left unsaid: *Abraham Hausman, father of two, husband of one, lives and works in Brooklyn, New York, which, if it weren't so nice, wouldn't be worth the embarrassing cliché. He writes books that touch on the American Jewish experience but were met with a shrug by both parents, dismissed as too Jewish by his mother and not Jewish enough by his father. Also his mother, who for the first part of her life found refuge in books, came to hate them for painting a world she finally entered but didn't recognize. So no wonder the writing, at first joyful, now feels like hard labor, the slightest cold parking Abe in front of the TV for hours, days even. His children bring him unquantifiable amounts of delight, and also fear, irritation, concern. Once his daughter asked whether, in a Sophie's Choice-type situation, she should pick her mother or father to live.*

Not only was this troubling in terms of the temperament and preoccupations of the questioner—but Abe didn't have an easy answer. Of course he should say she should choose his wife. But the truth was that Abe felt he would be better equipped to be alone. And, despite almost nauseating guilt, that maybe he would enjoy moving on. So he stayed silent. A reticence in life matched, perhaps, by verbosity on the page, an outlet Abe wonders if his quiet father could have used. Sometimes Abe wonders if his father would still be alive if he hadn't been lonely, one black hat in a sea of hats. Tales of his father's weakness persuade Abe that weakness lives in him too. In fact, he can sometimes be found practically luxuriating in it, most recently in the permission he's granted himself to fall in love with a movie star. And no—it's not what you're thinking. It's not just from an innocent distance . . . It's the real deal, the kind of connection you're lucky to find once in your life, if ever.

Anyway! Fellow alums, if you're ever in Brooklyn, give Abe a shout! Though chances are he doesn't really want to see you, or he'd have been in touch himself.

Beat.

Julia   I don't really know what to say. You've put me in an awkward position. I can't have you being in love with me.

Abe   Can you have me some other way then? I would just love to be had by you.

Sophie *enters.*

Sophie (*angrily*)   Abe, can I talk to you?

Abe   Right now?

Sophie   Yeah, right now!

Abe   Okay.

Sophie   Okay.

Abe   Okay.

It's as though now she doesn't know what to say.

Sophie   Actually . . . it can wait.

Abe (*truly asking*)   What's going on with you.

Sophie   What's going on with me?

Abe   Yeah.

Sophie   I don't know. You seem to think you have this monopoly on confusion—

Abe   I probably do think that, yeah.

Sophie   And I know—I know—I have these two living parents and so I'm very lucky but I think because of all your, your . . .

Abe   Tragedy, heartache, trauma.

Sophie   Yeah, because of all that—we don't ever focus on . . .

Abe   You.

Sophie   Right! Like yesterday? I was picking Esther up from school and again—again—someone mistakes me for a . . . I mean, the babysitter of this boy who's having a total meltdown, like he's literally tearing his clothes off *outside*— the babysitter, who's Black, turns to me and gives me this look like "they don't pay me enough for this shit" and then says, "Maybe I can switch with you?" because Esther is well-behaved . . . at least in public.

Abe   That doesn't mean that she—

Sophie   Trust me. But it's not that it happened, that it happens; it's how it makes me feel. Why on earth should it bother me so much? What am I so afraid of? And the other day my mother calls and she says she's thought about it and she doesn't like that you're sending the kids to Hebrew school; she says the Jews ostracized her and dad and that it's an insult to my father to send them. And I'm like "Is that what *Dad* thinks?"—a 75-year-old man from Mississippi who couldn't care less what the Jews think, and she says, "Yes even if he would never admit it." Which is . . . I mean, she will never acknowledge how crazy she is, probably because crazy people don't know they're crazy, but it's insane because it's not like I'm not . . . Jewish too. Ish. Maybe I'd like to send my kids to Hebrew school too!

Abe   Do you?

Sophie   No! But it's the principle. About how much she should intervene in our lives. And yeah, if my own work was . . . going better this other stuff might not matter so much but now it's . . . I mean, the problem is probably that I don't want to be any of the things that I actually am . . .

Abe (*not a dismissal; he's really trying*)   It sounds like you could use a drink, Soph.

Sophie   I could use a vacation.

Like maybe we should go somewhere and just . . . unplug.

Don't you think just getting away maybe? The two of us.

Abe   Maybe.

But I'm not sure I need to unplug.

Sophie   Well, I do.

Abe   We'll do it soon.

Sophie   When?

Abe   Soon.

Beat.

Sophie   Okay, I know you hate hearing my dreams—

Abe   When did I say that?

Sophie   It's the look on your face when I start to tell one. But last night I had this . . . Well, I dreamed an animal got into our house and disrupted it. Like you'd go into rooms and things weren't in the right places.

Abe   That sounds less like an animal than just the way we live.

Sophie   Well, then I went into the kids' room and they were sleeping, peacefully. Until I got closer and found that they'd been mauled in their beds.

Abe   God, Sophie.

Sophie   I know.

Abe   Don't have that dream again. Please.

Sophie   And when I woke up, you were gone.

Abe   I couldn't sleep so I went for a run.

Beat.

Sophie (*quietly*)   No . . . that's not what I meant.

Chapter Seven (or, The Visit)

Schmuli *appears on* **Esther**'s *doorstep. They stand facing each other. Neither knows what to say. It has been four years.*

Esther   What are you doing here?

Schmuli   How are you, Esther?

Esther   Fine.

Schmuli   Oh good! I'm very well too.

Esther   So we are all doing well then.

Schmuli   And this is your place. It's, um. Well. It's . . . Are here any windows?

Esther   Like where *we* were living was such a palace. Rivka will be down soon. She comes at nine to watch *Face the Nation*, so.

Schmuli   Where is Abraham? Is he home?

Esther   Where are my *girls*? Did you bring them?

Silence. **Schmuli** *is fiddling with his hat.*

Esther   Oh, just take it off already, Schmuli. Please.

Schmuli   It's something, Esther. To see you like this. I mean, your hair; it's . . .

Instinctively she reaches to cover it, realizing he's never seen her like this.

Schmuli (*with so much feeling*)   No, it's beautiful.

She is moved, and confused.

Esther (*this is all too much for her*)   I have to go. I'm sorry.

Schmuli   No, wait. Please wait. You think I didn't see you all those years. But I did. I saw you. I saw you when you ate something you disliked but tried to hide the unpleasantness. I heard you murmur in your sleep, asking always for your mother. I saw the way you looked at me, the way you look at me still, which is not with disgust, but with wistfulness, as though things could be different. With the affectionate frustration one reserves for one's children. You can't see yourself. I am telling you the look on your face.

Esther   The look on my face.

Schmuli   It's been years. I think you could be forgiven. I think I can forgive you.

Esther   What makes you think *I* could ever forgive *you*?

Schmuli   Are you happy here, Esther?

Esther   Abraham is a very bright boy. He excels in school. Already.

Schmuli   I brought him a present.

Esther   Why?

Schmuli (*with real emotion*)   It's his birthday today, *nu*? Don' you understand why I'm here? It's been long enough. Four years, Esther. I miss my son. I feel him like this gaping hole in my . . .

He hands her a wrapped present.

Will you give it to him?

Esther (*drily*)   What is it? The Gemara?

Schmuli   *The Collected Stories of Winnie the Pooh.*

Esther   Oh.

Schmuli   I read it. It is a story a father tells his son.

Esther   I don't know what to say.

Schmuli   Life isn't the same without you. Home isn't the same without you.

Esther (*quietly, reflective*)   . . . I dream about it, you know. The way you wake up on Fridays and the air feels different. Everything closed by noon and the women scurrying for challah, for fish, for wine. The flurry of hats and coats on Marcy Avenue, rushing to be home before dark. And the birthdays and the holidays . . . and the way no one is forgotten. Everyone suspended together over all the years that have passed and all the years to come in a song that will never end.

Schmuli   . . . I knew you'd be trouble from the moment I agreed to marry you. You'd rejected all those matches, good men too: Schlomo Lipsky, Chezky Blankenstok, Dovid Mendelbaum.

Esther   You knew about that?

Schmuli   It's what clinched it for me. Why I had to have you. And why I need you still. See, I will not remarry. You are my *bashert*. The only one for me. A woman with her own mind. A skeptic.

Esther (*quietly*)   But that's the thing. I don't think my mind works right, Schmuli.

Schmuli   Why do you say that?

Esther I thought when I got out of Brooklyn, it would be as though the bars had lifted. But it turns out they are inside me. That I am looking for life to give me something it will never provide.

Schmuli Which is what?

Esther That's the problem. I'm not sure.

Schmuli Oh my *liebling*. Come home now. It's not like I have it all figured out. It's not like I don't have doubts.

Esther So, what. You are suggesting we just . . . change nothing? And I simply come back with you?

Schmuli Is this not a change? It is your choice.

(*With real feeling.*) I have . . . given over to you.

Back to **Abe** *and* **Julia**, *instant messaging.*

Julia Do you ever think, if you had it all to do over again, you'd undo anything?

Abe Anything? I'd undo everything.

Julia No you wouldn't.

Abe I would. I thought you would know that about me, by now.

Julia I don't even think I really know my own *husband*. Isn't that insane?

Abe Sometimes, when I've been out all day, I get home and Sophie literally has her hands over her ears. I'm not sure if she's shutting me out, or the kids. Or both.

Julia Sometimes it gets to be too much. You imagine living other lives.

Abe (*matter-of-fact*) That's called being a person, Julia.

Julia I think maybe knowing you has made me sadder than I was before.

Abe (*chuckling*)   You're not the first woman to have said that
to me.

Julia   Does Sophie . . . is she happier than you are?

Abe   Well that's a pretty low bar. So yes—even if she's been
a little distracted lately. And by lately I mean the last decade
or so. But I can't expect her to be enchanted by me forever.
Really she's been generous. She hasn't gotten all the things
she wanted.

Julia   She sounds wonderful, and patient.

Abe   She hasn't left me yet.

Julia   I feel that way about James. Like why hasn't he fled
so many times?

Abe   Do you want your marriage upended?

Julia   Why, should we run off together?

Long beat.

Abe   I don't know. Probably.

Beat.

But then we'd be in the less than ideal position of having to
trust someone who just proved him or herself patently
untrustworthy.

Also there *are* the children to think of.

Which makes me sound like a character in a Russian novel.

Julia (*surprised*)   You've really thought about this.

Abe   Sometimes Sophie talks about having another baby.

Julia   Well . . . it's not for the faint of heart. And I say that
as someone whose babies both routinely required three
people to change their diapers. So vast was the mess. It
would hit the walls, Abe.

Abe   Also, all I can think about sometimes is having a baby with you.

Julia (*quietly*)   You do?

Abe   What he would look like. That we would name him after my father. His artistic pedigree that would send him right into the sciences . . . That our lives would be officially intertwined. That it would be awfully fun to make a baby with you.

Julia (*impulsive, out of nowhere*)   Abe, do you prefer me to your wife?

Beat.

Abe   Well, that's a deeply unfair question.

Julia   Is it?

Abe   There's so much I don't know about you. Whereas I've known Sophie forever. She's practically an extension of me.

Julia   You *really* think you know everything about her?

Abe   More or less.

Julia   Do you think she knows everything about you?

Abe   She's seen me through so much. So yes. But are there things I keep from her? . . . Sure.

Julia   Such as.

Abe   Oh, I don't know . . . Probably the same things I keep from myself.

Julia   What do you keep from yourself? You can tell me.

Beat.

Abe   I'll set a scene for you: Seventh grade. My mother was having terrible nightmares about my grandfather coming to kidnap me. The dreams were so bad we kept all the lights on, in every room, at all times. But on this particular day, when I got home from basketball practice I found my mother sitting completely still on the couch in total darkness. I went up to her, "Are you okay, *Mameh*?" And out of the darkness, her voice, and I remember it as being filled with an almost childlike wonder, said: "Abraham, I've just realized that you are my only reason for being alive." And then she said it again . . . year after year after year after year. Until, at a certain point, I guess I stopped being a good enough reason.

Julia   You think you disappointed your mother, don't you. Let her down. You'll never let that go.

Abe   No I disappointed my *father*. When I was an adult I ignored virtually all of his attempts to get in touch, or to see me. And all he'd ever wanted was a son. So yeah, him I let down. I *killed* my mother.

Julia   No you didn't, Abe.

Abe   You're a nice person, Julia, and you say nice things. But when a person exterminates herself, there's an inescapable truth at the center of it all.

Julia   Which is?

Abe   They could have been saved.

Julia   That's just not always true.

Abe   It's incontrovertibly true. If someone else hadn't been selfish, they could have been saved . . .

I'll explain: I was on my book tour in San Diego, for *Orphan*—which is of course richly ironic.

Julia   Why is that ironic?

Abe   Because I spent years of my life, Julia, years when my parents were both *alive*, toiling over this book about a fucking *orphan*.

Julia   Don't do that to yourself. You didn't know what was coming.

Abe So there I am standing in front of Barnes and Noble, having just read from that stupid book, when my mother calls and says, "I need you to come home, Abraham." My sister Leah had just had her third baby and my mother was desperate to be there. Each baby my sisters had was another huge blow, each one a reminder of everything my mother didn't have. But I was a week away from the end of the tour. And this wasn't the first time she'd asked this of me. So I told her she would have to wait. I said one week, *Mameh*. And I hung up.

Julia You've never told me this part of the story.

Abe Sophie doesn't even know it. How could I tell her? You see, my mother begged me to marry her. For years, she *begged* me. She loved Soph like she was her own daughter and my mother was tragically short on family for someone who so badly wanted it. She was unsubtle about it. (*With a slight Yiddish lilt.*) "Abraham, you're going to marry that girl; you want to even if you don't know it yet." She was a Jewish mother, whether she liked it or not. She was also my mother. My only mother.

Beat.

I got the call when I was on the train, somewhere between San Diego and L.A. My phone buzzed in my pocket and I knew. I did. I knew. So I didn't pick up. This was one of the many times I didn't answer when my father called.

I flew home. I took a cab from the airport straight to Williamsburg, straight to Sophie. It was the middle of the night. I walked up those five flights of stairs and banged on the door until she let me in. And she let me in because I let her believe I was who she wanted me to be. She let me in because she was genuinely in love with me, which is actually the hardest thing to . . . But how could I not be with her? How could I not have those children my mother so desperately wanted? Every book I ever write will be a *mea culpa*. Every word a reminder of that particular cruelty. No, *everything* is a reminder. The days I spend in front of blank screens when I should be . . . I mean, my kids are growing so fast I hardly recognize them. And I just . . . I don't want anyone else to die. Please. Don't let anyone else . . . I can't do it. I can't tell my wife I didn't love her the way she loved me, that I *submitted* to our marriage. I don't even want to believe it. Could there be anything sadder? But the saddest things are usually true. My mother in the darkness. The way when I look at my wife I feel such shame. You understand now.

Silence. Then we see **Julia** *exit.*

Abe   Julia? Are you there?

Julia?

Sophie *appears in the doorway.*

Sophie   Oh, I'm here all right.

Abe (*quietly*)   What's going on?

Sophie   What's going on is that you just said you never loved me.

Abe   I don't . . . What do you . . . Wait.

Sophie   Why would you say that, Abe? I mean, you do love me. I know you do.

Abe   Of course I love you.

Sophie (*dawning on her*)   Or maybe you don't. Maybe you really don't. And never did. Maybe you literally never loved me.

(*Then, really hitting her.*) Oh my God.

Abe   Soph, Sophie . . . where is this all coming from? I'm not quite . . .

Sophie   I feel like such a . . . I just thought it was a game. I don't know why I thought it was a game. I mean: "Reading your email was like hearing my name called while walking down a street in a foreign country where I didn't think anyone knew me."

Beat.

Abe   Please, Sophie. I don't understand.

Sophie   And you don't know me at all, Abe.

The way you describe me. A little patient woman. Poor Sophie. Who doesn't like being such a failure but tolerates it because what else can you do.

Abe   I never said that.

Sophie   You said worse.

Abe   I'm just . . . I'm . . . I can't wrap my head around . . .

Sophie   The night of that reading. You couldn't stop talking about how she was there. Julia Cheever. Could I believe it? Like seeing a beloved character in real life. It messes with your equilibrium. Your sense of what's real and not real.

Abe   I still can't believe she came to that reading. I still can't believe that she wrote me. That she kept writing to me.

Sophie   But she never wrote to you, Abe. Not even once.

Beat.

Abe   Not even once.

Sophie   That night . . . the night of the reading . . . I saw something in you I hadn't seen in a long time. It took me a while to realize what it was, but then I did: How much you wanted to impress her. And I saw how little you care about impressing me. Not that I can blame you. It's old hat, impressing me. But I wanted to know what that felt like— not to feel wanted by you, though there is that, of course, but to feel worthy of your making an effort. So I'll admit: It started off as a little joke because you were just *so* bowled over to have seen her that night. You couldn't stop talking about it. But then you got so into it. And I got so into it.

Abe   God. Sophie.

Sophie   And I got this little taste of what it must be to feel important. To feel like a success in the world. It's heady.

Abe   Please no. Anything but this.

Sophie   Anything but this. I agree.

Abe (*dawning on him*)   Hundreds—no, thousands—of messages. Every single one a lie.

Sophie   And you don't think you were lying to me?

Abe   I *was* lying to you. But in a less fucked-up way.

Sophie   I would dispute that.

Abe   You deliberately set this trap for me.

Sophie   It was sort of like dating you again. It was addictive. But then you sold out our marriage so completely for this fantasy—

Abe   You wanted me to! For some sick reason you wanted me to!

Sophie   You said you wanted to have a baby with this woman! A baby, Abe. Can you imagine how that would sound to me? When you've made *me* feel like an asshole for even bringing it up.

Abe   I can't imagine any of this. It is literally unimaginable to me.

Sophie   How long would you have let it go on for? Forever?

Abe   I don't know. Maybe! But you tricked me. You manipulated me. You got me to say exactly what you wanted me to say.

Sophie   That your dead mother forced you to marry me? That you never loved me? That's what I wanted to hear?

Abe   You wanted me to see things I didn't wanna see. And then I did. I *saw* them. And now here we are . . .

I mean, you let her console me after my father died!

Sophie   Well, you didn't want *me* to! And it seemed to help.

Abe   Help?! It was a fiction, Sophie. All a fiction! Why would you do this? Why would you push me into this woman's arms?

Sophie   It didn't take much pushing.

Abe (*realizing*)   You enjoyed it, didn't you . . . You fucking enjoyed it!

Sophie   I just thought it would become obvious to you at some point. And it never did.

Abe   You're a good writer, Sophie.

Sophie   I don't think I enjoyed it. I got stomachaches. Sometimes I felt like I couldn't breathe.

Abe   So you knew how wrong it was. See? You knew.

Sophie   And so did you, Abe. You knew too.

Beat.

Abe (*this is impossibly sad*)   This is . . . I mean, Sophie. Everything about this.

Sophie (*this is unbearable too*)   I wish you could have come to me about your mom's . . . I mean, I *am* sorry that you feel so responsible for her, um . . . I don't think you should.

Abe   But I did go to you. I went right to you. Right to your doorstep. And you took me in.

Sophie   I did.

Abe (*begging her not to*)   You can't leave me over this. You wouldn't. I mean, what I did was terrible; it was undeniably wrong but if I was having an affair, or something like an affair, wasn't it . . . with you?

Sophie   . . . Was it? I don't know what I know anymore. But I don't buy that our marriage was arranged, Abe. I really don't. We chose each other . . . I think what we're seeing now is that it wasn't the right choice.

Chapter Eight (or, Fiction)

Lights shift. **Schmuli** *is outside in the snow;* **Esther** *in the doorway, between worlds.*

Schmuli   Esther!

Esther!

Come out here!

It's delicious.

It's beautiful.

It's bracing.

Just look into the sky.

Esther   Oh Schmuli, it's too cold. I'll stay here.

Schmuli   No, you have to come. Come on, *mommellah*.

It's nice. It makes you feel alive.

And for once I don't feel too warm.

For once I'm not *shvitzing*.

She starts to go to him.

That's right, Esther. "Come to me."

She smiles, despite herself.

Esther   I'm not sure I like it.

I need boots.

I feel the wet in my socks.

Schmuli   If it is unpleasant it will make the warming-up later all the sweeter.

Esther   Who died and made you a philosopher, Schmuli Simcha.

Schmuli   No one has died, my love.

No one will die.

A pause. A breath. **Abe** *enters. We are online. At least a year later.*

Abe   Julia?

Are you there?

Are you there, Julia?

Sophie *enters.*

Abe   Oh there you are.

Julia Cheever, right?

This is Tom Brokaw.

It's nice to meet you.

Beat.

Sophie (*playing along but wary*)   Tom. Can it really be you?

Abe   It's me. I came straight from speaking at a convention of members of the greatest generation. They were all dead so it didn't take long.

Sophie   So no stage fright.

Abe   You'd think, but actually it was brutal. The dead really are very judgmental.

Sophie   So . . . what are you doing here?

Abe   I came looking for you.

Sophie   Abe.

Abe   Tom.

Sophie   Fine. Tom.

Abe   I've always thought you were so cute. If I didn't have such a wonderful, supportive family in the heart of the Midwest I might lie down at your feet.

Sophie   Okay, I'm not sure where the fantasy ends and the reality begins here.

Abe   Isn't that always true?

Sophie   How are you, Abe?

Abe   Oh, about as well as an orphaned soon to be divorcee with children suddenly old enough to walk themselves to school can be expected to be. Why we didn't have another kid when we had the chance I'll never know.

Sophie   Are you joking? I can't tell if you're joking.

Abe   Of course it's possible that we've made a real mess of the ones we already have.

Sophie   Well, Robby was assigned a book report this week— he could write about anything—the Yankees, polar bears, anything—and he's writing it on *Schindler's List*, so yeah: Maybe.

Abe   Yup, irretrievably ruined.

Sophie   You know, I actually think they're doing okay, considering.

Abe   That should be my epitaph: He did okay, considering.

Or the title of my new book.

Which I finished, by the way. I hoped I could share it with you.

Sophie   Oh, I don't know, Abe.

Abe   "I don't know, Abe; you're awesome—and actually I really do think I'd like to read it."

Sophie   Ha ha.

Abe   It's not what you think . . . I don't even know if it's for . . . general consumption. I really just want to show it to you.

Sophie   Only me.

Abe   It's about my parents.

Sophie   Okay.

Abe   All I can think of is my father dying alone. The snow in his beard, and no one beside him. I can't get that image . . . I couldn't have it end that way.

Sophie   So you rewrote the ending?

Abe   Now they end up together. In Albany, in the depths of winter. At that house on Amy Lane, with the always broken front porch light. Only now my father has fixed it.

Sophie   Did it make you feel better?

Abe   It feels as real to me as if it truly happened.

Isn't that odd?

Sophie   No I don't think so.

Abe   So you'll read it?

Sophie   . . . I'm not sure. I'll think about it.

Abe   Thank you for thinking about it.

Sophie   You know I finished my book too.

Abe   Sophie, that's amazing.

Sophie   It is. And I think it's really good.

Abe   There is no doubt in my mind.

Sophie   There is, but that's okay. It doesn't matter. It's about me. Us. It's memoir-*ish*.

Abe   What's it called?

Sophie   *The Wanderers*, maybe.

Abe   I like it. The Jews in the desert for forty years.

Sophie   Sort of. Or just the idea of it. That it can take a lifetime just to grow up. To let go of a certain sort of galvanizing restlessness that leaves you always empty.

Happy birthday, by the way. Belatedly.

Abe   Thank you. Though "happy" doesn't really apply at a certain point, does it?

Sophie   I think it can. I think it should. For our whole lives, it should.

Abe *is at a loss.*

Abe   Do you wanna know how I spent it, my birthday? It's kinda crazy. You won't believe it.

Sophie   Try me.

Abe   So I was at this Rockefeller Foundation gala.

Sophie   Okay, this is really stretching my disbelief.

Abe   No, wait. It was in London. A special anniversary event.

Beat.

Sophie   In London. How'd you get there?

Abe   I flew.

Sophie   And you weren't scared?

Abe   I was terrified. But I guess I put my faith in God, or something like God.

Sophie   Really?

Abe   And as the plane rose into the sky, I prayed. Mostly for forgiveness. *Avinu Malkeinu.* Hear our voice. *Avinu Malkeinu.* Have compassion on us, on our parents and on our children. *Avinu Malkeinu.* Inscribe us for blessing in the book of life.

And then I emerged from the plane and found my way into that beautiful city where holiday lights hung in every window and the snow-covered sidewalks were illuminated by streetlamps like it could have been two hundred years ago and I was filled with this . . . ecstasy I guess.

Sophie (*genuine*)   Wow. Good for you.

Abe   And at the gala, there were readings. Alice Munro. Ian McEwan. Toni Morrison. And then Philip Roth's up there and he reads a little excerpt from *Portnoy*.

Sophie   No shit.

Abe   And who do you think is in the front row but . . .

Sophie (*quietly*)   Julia Cheever.

Abe   Ding, ding, ding. And after Roth reads, she raises her hand and asks how he would characterize himself—is he Jewish first, or a man, or an American. Or an asshole . . . Or an artist.

Sophie   What did he say?

Abe   He said . . . There is nothing I could say that would not be a fiction except that I am first and last the product of my parents.

Sophie   Huh.

Abe   And after the reading she sees me.

Sophie   Was it because you were standing two feet away staring at her?

Abe   Hilarious, Sophie. No, I wasn't. But she literally came up to me and was like:

Julia *enters.*

Julia   Is that Abraham Hausman?

Abe   That is.

Julia   This is so funny.

Abe   Is it?

Julia   I've been hoping to meet you. You gave a reading a few years back at Book Court—in Brooklyn.

Abe   You were there. In the front row. I remember.

Julia   Wow. I wondered if you'd seen me. Not to be immodest or anything.

Abe   No, be immodest. If I were you I'd be immodest too.

Julia   Well, I just wanted to let you know I'm a big fan.

Abe   As I am of yours.

Julia   I think your writing is sort of . . . luminous.

Abe   I don't know what to say.

Julia   What are you working on these days?

Abe   Oh just, basically, trying to heal the gaping chasm in my marriage and my life that my wife pretending to be you writing to me for a year and a half created.

Back to **Sophie**.

Abe   And did she laugh.

Sophie   You didn't really say that to her.

Abe   I did.

Sophie   . . . You really are something, Tom Brokaw.

Abe   I know. That's just how we roll in the not quite greatest generation.

And then—get this—she told me she'd like to be in touch. Maybe she could pitch *A Theory of Milk* around L.A., get a "long-overdue"—her words—adaptation underway. And I politely declined.

Sophie   You did?

Abe   Yeah.

Sophie   Well, that was idiotic because we could use the money.

Abe   You're joking.

Sophie   Only half.

Abe   Not a problem. We can add it to my prodigious inventory of mistakes and accidents. From the accident of my birth all the way up to however I will manage to botch this crucial communication with my *bashert* . . . (*As open/ vulnerable as he's ever been.*) The only one for me . . . The real deal.

Sophie *sighs.*

Abe   I can feel you sighing through the computer.

Sophie   Can you?

Abe   I can feel it all. Sophie.

Beat.

Sophie   So I had a dream last night.

Abe   Oh no, please not a repeat of the one about our children getting mauled.

Sophie   No. In this one, Robby was little again.

He sleepwalked into the living room, where we were sitting in the bright light, and lay down on the couch next to us as though we weren't there at all. His breath moved gently through him. His palms were face up, like a little supplicant, only it wasn't clear what he wanted. Outside it was snowing, and it seemed, in that moment, like he might be small forever.

And then you scooped him up, like in a picture book, and carried him back to his room, this baby we once had, your lips pressed to his forehead the whole way.

Beat. **Abe** *is crying.*

Sophie   That was it. That was my dream. Or maybe it's a memory. I'm not sure there's any difference.

Abe   I don't . . .

I don't have any words.

Sophie   I think that's okay. Abe.

Abe   *Ein ba'al ha-nes makir b'niso.*

Sophie.

Sophie (*gently*)   What does that mean?

Breath. The rest of the stage opens up, like a camera angle widening.

Esther   Schmuli, I'm freezing my *tuchus* off!

Schmuli   Good!

Esther   I'm not happy.

Schmuli   That's okay. Make an angel.

Esther   What?

Schmuli   Make an angel in the snow.

And then our children will come out and lie down in the space we have made for them.

Esther   I don't know if I can.

Schmuli   Esther.

Ein ba'al ha-nes makir b'niso.

Beat.

Esther   I know.

Schmuli   Let us feel how fortunate we are.

She looks at him and then, slowly, takes his hand.

The lights fade to black.

End of Play.